Booklinks

by Arlene S. Brown

©1993

ECS *Learning Systems* INC.

Printed in the U.S.A.

Editors: Lori Mammen and Jennifer Knoblock
Page Layout & Graphics: Kathryn Riches
Cover/Book Design: Educational Media Services

Other Titles from ECS Learning Systems, Inc.

ECS9072	Writing Warm-Ups™	(Grades K-6)
ECS9080	Writing Warm-Ups™	(Grades 7-12)
ECS9455	Writing Warm-Ups™ Two	(Grades K-6)
ECS9463	Writing Warm-Ups™ Two	(Grades 7-12)
ECS9439	Tactics to Tackle Thinking Creative Activities for the English Classroom	(Grades 7-12)
ECS947-1	Quick Thinking™	(Grades K-6)
ECS948-X	Quick Thinking™	(Grades 7-12)
ECS951X	Building Language Power Book I	(Grades 4-9)
ECS9528	Building Language Power Book II	(Grades 4-9)
ECS9498	Springboards for English	(Grades 6-12)
ECS9609	Inkblots A Creative Writing Syllabus	(Grades 6-12)

To order, contact your local school supply store, or write/call:

ECS Learning Systems, Inc.
P.O. Box 791437
San Antonio, Texas 78279-1437
1-800-68-TEACH

ISBN 0-944459-61-7

Copyright 1993 by ECS Learning Systems, Inc., San Antonio, Texas. All rights reserved. No part of this publication may be reproduced, stored in a retrieval system, or transmitted in any way or by any means (electronic, mechanical, photocopying, recording, or otherwise) without prior written permission from ECS Learning Systems, Inc., with the exceptions found below.

Reproduction of worksheets in any manner for use in a classroom and not for commercial sale is permissible.

Reproduction of these materials for an entire school, or for a school system, is strictly prohibited.

Table of Contents

Introduction — 4

Reader Links — 5

Setting Links — 23

Character Links — 29

Plot Links — 63

Sentence Links — 81

Introduction

This book comes from my years of teaching reading and writing with the best of children's literature. The assignments are versatile enough to use in many classroom situations—from each child reading in a different book, to small literature groups, to the whole class on the same page at the same time. In recognition of teachers' valuable time, the instructions are simple and straightforward. Teachers can come in the morning, reproduce a page for students, and have an instant writing lesson linked to their reading program, regardless of its diversity. When giving instructions to the class, teachers can make expectations clearer by illustrating them with incidents from the book students are reading or hearing read aloud. Teachers also might choose a book or story which everyone knows, such as a favorite fairy tale. At the end of the reading-writing period, teachers will have some concrete evidence of their students' abilities.

These pages are sparsely illustrated; many have empty spaces. Teachers might suggest that students fill the spaces with a form of expression important to them. Some will want to doodle while thinking about their writing. Others may feel their work is not finished until it is decorated with something beautiful.

This book was made for teachers and their students to enjoy reading-writing-art. I hope they will use it to their best purposes—and have a good time doing it.

Reader Links

Title~

Author~

Open a book that is unfamiliar to you. Looking only at the pictures, what do you think the subject of the book will be?

Title~
Author~

Choose a book that is unfamiliar to you. Without opening it, learn as much as you can by looking at the covers. Write your observations here.

Will it be worth your time and effort to read this book? Why?

Title~

Author~

Fold a piece of construction paper in half. On the inside write about your favorite book, telling what it's all about. On the outside, design a new cover for it. Plan your cover in the space below.

Title~
Author~

In four short sentences, tell about the most important things you read today.

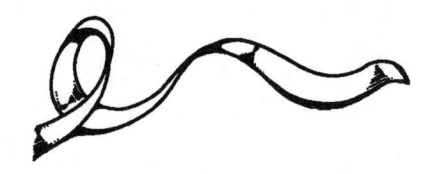

In your opinion, what makes a book worth reading?

How do you find a book that is worth reading?

Title~

Author~

Have you ever read a book that changed your life or at least the way you do some things? How did the book change your life? You may explain the change in words or pictures.

Title~

Author~

What do you know how to do that you could teach to someone in the book you're reading?

List three of your friends. What books do you think they'd like to read? Why?

Title~
Author~

As a student, you have read many books. Which book will you remember best when you are an adult? Why?

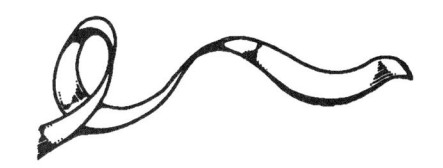

Pretend you're twenty-five years old. What kind of reading do you think you'll be doing then? How much will you read because you must? What will you read for fun? How will your reading differ from the kind you do now?

Title~
Author~

Characters in books often do things we wish we could do. Which character from your book has done something that you would like to do? What did the character do?

Will you ever get to do it? Why?

Title~
Author~

Authors love to hear from the people who read their work. Write a letter to the author of your favorite book telling him/her why you liked the story so much, what parts you found most interesting—or exciting—or funny—or touching. Which characters did you like the best, and why? Tell something about yourself, too. Maybe you'll find yourself in the author's new book.

You may mail the letter to the author in care of the company that published the book. The address of that company is almost always found on the back of the title page.

Title~
Author~

If you like one book by an author, you will probably like other books the author has written. Read another book by the same author. What do you notice about the second book that reminds you of the first book? Are there any similarities in style, plot, or characters? Are there any differences?

Did you like both books equally well? Why?

Title~

Author~

Cut a bookmark from a heavy piece of paper. On the paper write the name of the book you've read and the author's name. Then write a sentence or two that will stir the interest of the next person who selects the book. Add a little decoration. Leave it in the book for the next reader to use. You may plan the bookmark in the space below.

Title~

Author~

Design a magazine ad for the book you're reading. Give the title and the author's name an important place in the ad. Draw pictures of the characters. Write something about the book that will interest other readers and encourage them to buy a copy.

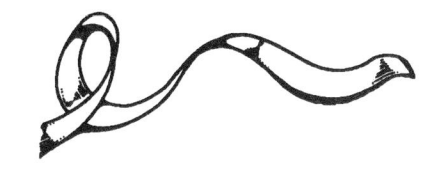

Keep an annotated bibliography on a set of blank index cards. Each time you finish a book, complete a card for it. Write the author's name, last name first. Write the title. Write one sentence that summarizes the book. Keep your cards in alphabetical order by the authors' last names.

Author:

Title:

One-sentence summary:

Notes

Setting Links

Title~

Author~

Draw the setting from a scene in your book. Write a few sentences telling what happened there.

Title~
Author~

People's rooms tell a lot about their personalities. Pretend you're looking into the room of a character from your book. Describe the room. Does the character share it with someone? Is it neat or messy? What kinds of pictures, maps, books, toys, or awards are on display?

Describe your room.

Title~

Author~

If your story unfolds in a real place, find that place on a map. What passages in the book tell you where the story is happening?

Title~
Author~

Some stories happen in a place that is not real. They happen in a fictional place. How does the author describe what this place is like?

Does the author give enough clues to find a real location on a map for the make-believe place in the story? Why or why not?

Title~
Author~

The setting of a story is the time and place where everything happens. Setting is essential to every story. If you changed the setting of the story you're reading, how would it affect the characters and the events? For example, if Cinderella lived in your town today, she might call herself "Cindy" and have her own house cleaning business. She'd probably get her own apartment to escape from her nagging stepsisters.

Character Links

Title~
Author~

Write an Acrostic poem. Write the name of a book character vertically on the left side of the paper. Now, write a word or short phrase using each letter of the name as the first letter of a new word. Try to think of words that fit the character's personality.

Try it with your own name.

Title~

Author~

Draw two characters from your story. Write what they are saying to each other in the balloons.

© 1993 by ECS Learning Systems, Inc., San Antonio, Texas   All rights reserved

Title~
Author~

A blueprint is a map of a house and is drawn in white on blue paper. Draw a blueprint of the house where one of your book's characters lives. You'll need a separate blueprint for each floor in the character's house. Use neat printing to identify each room. Practice here before using good paper. Can you make a blueprint of your house?

Title~

Author~

Many people state their opinions on buttons. Draw someone from your book around this button. Then write the character's opinion on the button.

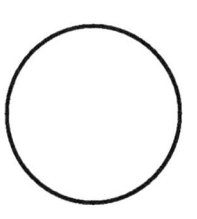

Title~

Author~

Draw some of the minor characters in your book. They are watching some of the more important characters.

What are the important characters doing?

Title~

Author~

Draw a picture of a character from your book. Write a few sentences telling what this character looks like.

Title~
Author~

A medieval knight used a coat of arms on his shield so he could be identified in a battle. Design a coat of arms for a character in your book. Include things that are so special to the character that the coat of arms could not belong to anyone else in the book. You may put animals, plants, or symbols around the shield as well as inside it. Then write a few sentences telling why you chose these things to represent this character.

Title~
Author~

Draw the faces of three characters from your book. Make their expressions clearly show how they are feeling.

Why do the characters feel the way they do?

Title~

Author~

Award a trophy to someone in your book. How did the character earn the trophy? What does the trophy look like?

Title~
Author~

Pretend you are a character from your book. Without giving your name, write sentences about yourself. Describe yourself. Tell some of the things you do. Tell some of the things that have happened to you.

Read your description, one sentence at a time, to your classmates. How long do you think it will take them to guess who you are?

Title~
Author~

If you could become a character in a book, which book would it be?

How would your presence change the final outcome of the story?

Title~

Author~

List or sketch some ways in which the main character's life is the same as your life. Then list or sketch some ways in which the main character's life is different from your life.

Same	Different

Title~

Author~

Think for a minute. Which things do you like best about your friends? Write them here.

Which of these qualities have you found in a character from a book? Explain your answer.

Do you think you could be friends with this character? Why or why not?

Title~

Author~

Pretend you are phoning a character from your book. Write the conversation you would have with the character.

Title~

Author~

There is something in this box that a character from your book wants very much. Who is it? What's in the box? Why does the character think it's so important?

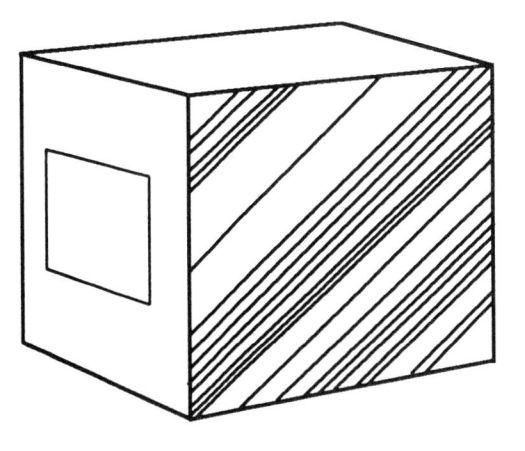

Title~

Author~

Whose life is easier—your life, or the life of the main character in the book you're reading? Explain.

Title~
Author~

Pretend you are the teacher of a character from your book. Complete a progress report for the character.

Name of student

Language
Teacher's comments

Mathematics
Teacher's comments

Physical Education
Teacher's comments

Art & Music
Teacher's comments

Social Growth
Teacher's comments

Title~

Author~

Pretend you are having a party for one of the characters in your book. Make a guest list (real people and characters from your book).

Menu

Music

Games

Title~

Author~

Design a beautiful party invitation. Write where and when the party will take place. Be sure to tell the guests why the character in your book is being honored with a party.

Title~

Author~

Most people like to be told when they're doing well. Create an award for a character in your book. Tell what good thing this person has done and why (s)he is being honored. Leave room for a seal and a ribbon. Make a fancy border. Plan your award in the space below.

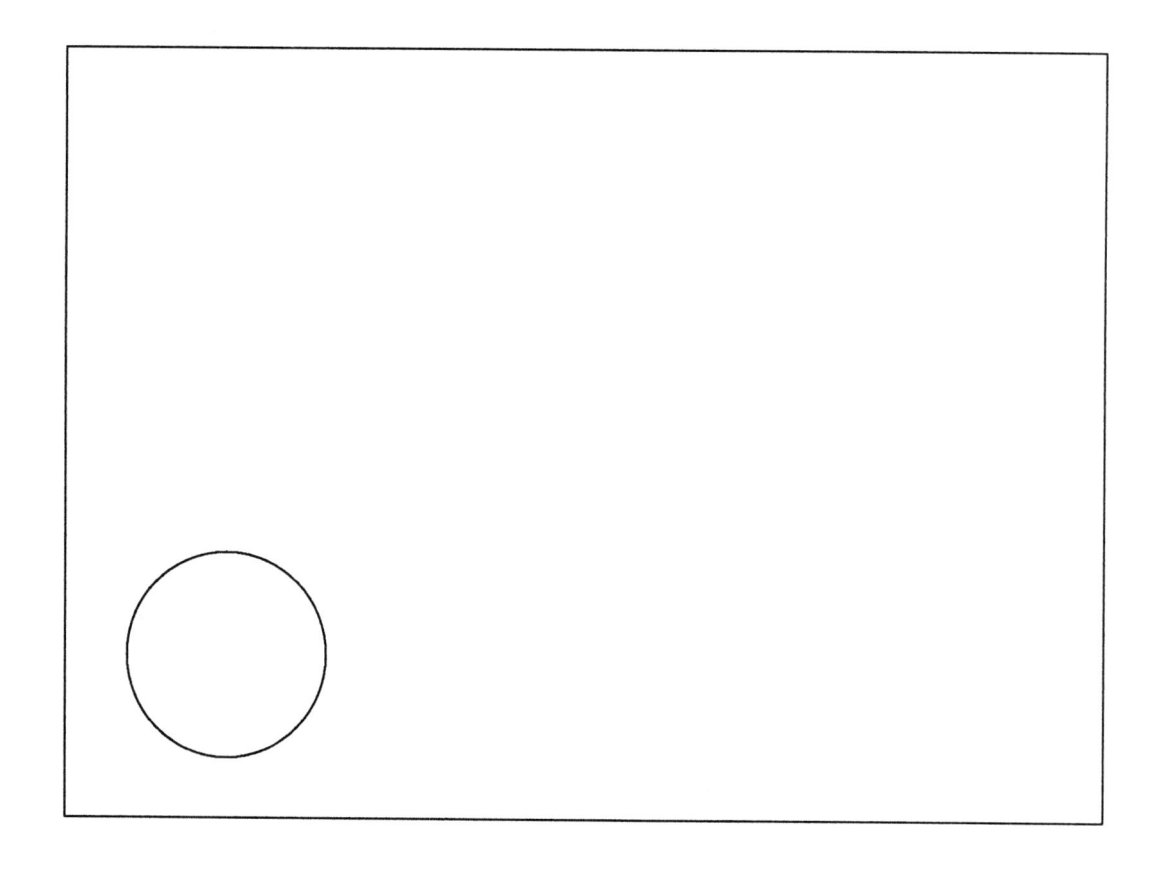

Title~
Author~

List ten things you really like about a character in the book you're reading.

Title~

Author~

Who is the nicest person in your book?

What events or people in this character's life probably made him/her so nice?

Title~
Author~

Who is the meanest person in your book?

What events or people in this character's life probably made him/her so mean?

Title~

Author~

Pretend that you are the main character in your book. Write how you feel about some of the other characters in the story.

Title~

Author~

Which people have the most influence on the main character of your book? How do they affect his/her actions and decisions?

Title~

Author~

A hobby is something you do because you like doing it. What kinds of hobbies do the characters in your book have?

What are your hobbies? Why do you enjoy them?

Title~
Author~

Pay a compliment to each of three characters in your book. Explain why you're saying these nice things to them.

Title~

Author~

If a character in your book wrote to an advice columnist and asked for help with a problem, what would the letter say?

Title~

Author~

If you were an advice columnist, what advice would you write to a character who's having problems?

Title~
Author~

Choose a character from your book and explain what you think the character's life will be like ten years from now. Explain your reasons for this prediction.

Title~

Author~

Many people keep diaries. They write their thoughts, feelings, and secrets, or they simply record the events of the day. Pretend that you are a character in a book and write a page for your diary. Tell about the kind of day you've had.

Dear Diary,

Title~

Author~

You must have met a character in a book who reminded you of yourself, or of someone you know. Who was it? Compare the character to yourself or the person you know.

Plot Links

Title~

Author~

Draw a map showing where the most important events in your story take place. Put in natural features, such as rivers, lakes, and forests. Add cultural features, such as houses, schools, airports, and roads. Remember, a map is the way you would see things if you were in a plane looking down. You'd see the roofs of buildings and roads would look flat.

Title~

Author~

Create your own comic strip. Draw, in sequence, the series of events in your story. Have the characters speak their words in balloons like this.

Title~

Author~

Our favorite books are often made into movies or television plays. Some movies are faithful to the original, but many change the events in the book. Movie makers try to make the stories funnier, more exciting, or more interesting than the original. Have you ever seen this happen to a book that you have read? Did you like the changes? Do you think the changes were fair to the author? Why or why not?

Title~
Author~

Pretend you are a reporter for your local television station. Interview an eyewitness to an event that happened in your book.

Title~
Author~

Have you ever had to change your plans because of the weather? Choose an event in your book and change the weather. If things are happening on a sunny day, make it rain. If they take place in winter, change it to spring or summer. How does the weather change affect the course of the story? For example, if Cinderella's coach had stuck in the mud in a downpour, she might not have arrived at the palace—and the prince might have married someone else.

Title~

Author~

Write a prologue to your book. Tell what you think happened before the opening chapter.

Title~

Author~

Write about an event in your book. Don't tell how it was resolved. Give your paper to a friend and ask him/her to write an original ending.

Title~
Author~

Most stories are told from the main character's point of view. Choose a minor character from your book and retell the story from that character's point of view. For example: Perhaps Cinderella was a goody-two-shoes and simply drove her poor stepmother over the edge!

Title~
Author~

In only five sentences, write the sequence of events from a scene in your book. Cut the sentences apart and mix them up. See if a friend can put them in order. Be careful not to use words like first, or then, or next. That would give too many clues.

Title~

Author~

Can you tell a story in one line, the way the newspapers do? Cut a long strip of white paper. Use a black crayon or marker and print in capital letters. Write a headline about the most important events in your story. Remember that headlines try to catch the readers' attention so they'll be interested enough to read the whole story. For example,

MYSTERIOUS GLASS SLIPPER FOUND ON PALACE STEPS DURING BALL

Title~
Author~

If one of the characters in your book could have one wish, what do you think it would be? How would it change the course of the story?

Title~
Author~

As you read your book, keep a time line of the events as they happen. Don't go into much detail. Keep it simple, but in the order of things as they occur.

Title~

Author~

What do you think will happen to the people in your book now that the story is finished? Write a new chapter telling what everyone does next.

Title~
Author~

Make the events of your book into newspaper articles. Write separate articles for different happenings.

Remember that newspaper journalists try to answer
    who?
        what?
            where?
                when?
                    why?
                        in the very first paragraph.

Write the headlines with black marker. Have a special sports, business, or cooking section. Record the weather. Don't forget your by-line.

Title~
Author~

Pick two or more characters from your book and make them characters in a play. Have them talk about something that has happened in the story. Don't forget to set the scene. Be sure to give your play an original title.

If you'd like to make some finger puppets to go with your play, try this. Fold a tissue into thirds. Dip it into a mixture of one part water, and one part white glue. Mold it around your finger. In about ten minutes it will be firm enough to slip off your finger. Set it aside to dry for several hours. When it's dry, you can color it with markers or paints. You can make three or four finger puppets at the same time if you don't need your hands for awhile.

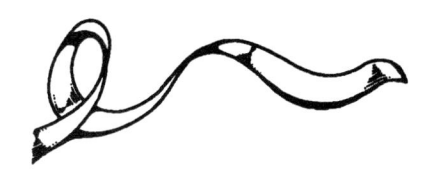

Title:

Author:

Scene:

Characters:

Title~
Author~

Make your own coloring book. For each chapter of the book you are reading, draw an outline picture of the most important event. Use a black marker or crayon. Under each picture write a caption of two or three sentences. When you're finished, put the pictures together as a book and give it to a friend to color. Plan some of your pictures in the space below.

Sentence Links

Title~

Author~

Write ten questions about your book. Your questions can be about people, places, events, ideas, or anything else about the story. You don't have to answer them.

Will you be able to answer them a month from now? A year from now?

Title~

Author~

A rebus is a sentence that uses pictures instead of words. The most famous rebus is probably

👁   (I)   ♥   (Love)   **U**   (You)

Write a summary of the book you've read, but write it as a rebus. Try to use as many pictures as you can.

Title~
Author~

Write five sentences about your reading. Leave an empty space for the most important word in the sentence. Under the space write the missing word with its letters scrambled. For example:

Cinderella's _____ was found by the prince.
                 prelips

Ask a friend to unscramble the words.

Title~

Author~

Make a word search. Choose ten interesting words from your reading. Write them on the lines; then write them in the boxes. Give the word search to a friend to solve. You may write the words across, down, or diagonally.

1.   6.

2.   7.

3.   8.

4.   9.

5.   10.

Word Search Puzzle

Title~

Author~

Find a word from your reading that you don't understand. Write it below. Reread the paragraph where the word appears. What do you think it means, given the way it's used in the story?

Ask someone who will know the meaning of the word, or check its meaning in the dictionary. Was your guess correct, or close to it? Try to use your new word in a sentence that will show you really understand it.

Title~

Author~

Choose ten interesting nouns from your reading. Write them below. Then write an entirely new story about your characters using at least five of the nouns.

Title~

Author~

Choose ten interesting adjectives from your reading. Write them below. Then write an entirely new story about your characters using at least five of the adjectives.

Title~

Author~

The Dadaists were a group of artists who saw art in accidental happenings. A Dada poem is fun to write. Choose ten verbs, eight nouns, a pronoun, a preposition, and a conjunction from your book. Write them in the boxes on the next page. Cut them apart and turn them over so you can't see the words. Mix the pieces. Now turn them right side up (one at a time) and arrange them in lines any way that looks good to you.

You've written a Dada poem. Copy it on paper and add some decorations.

Title~

Author~

"She sells sea shells by the sea shore" is a tongue twister. Use the name of a character in your book and write your own tongue twister. Start every word with the same first sound. Write another tongue twister using your own name.

Title~
Author~

Write five sentences about your story, but don't finish them. Give them to a friend and ask your friend to write the endings. Any ending will be fine, even if it's not the one in the book.

Title~

Author~

A fact is something that has really happened, something that is true. An opinion is a belief that is not necessarily true. Find three facts in your story.

Find three opinions in your story.

Notes

About the Author

Arlene S. Brown—

The author has lived close to the New England shore all her life, though her favorite place is the Arizona desert. One of the reasons she likes teaching so much is that it gives her an opportunity to read the many wonderful children's books that have been written since she was a child.